THE LONESOMEST SOUND
MIKE FERGUSON

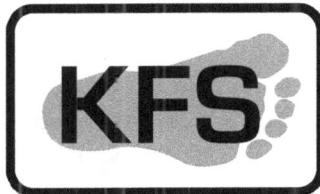

KFS

Newton-le-Willows

Published in the United Kingdom in 2020
by The Knives Forks And Spoons Press,
51 Pipit Avenue,
Newton-le-Willows,
Merseyside,
WA12 9RG.

ISBN 978-1-912211-55-5

Acknowledgements:

Poems have previously appeared in *82 Review; Adjacent Pineapple; Amaryllis; Anthropocene; Eunoia; Isacoustic; i am a silent poet; International Times; LossLit; M58; Mojave Heart Review; Perverse; Stride; The Honest Ulsterman; Train: a journal of prose poems - Issue #3; Train: a poetry journal; Turnpike Magazine; Unlost;* and *X-Peri.*

With thanks to those poetry magazine editors who have presented a number of these found prose poems; to Alec Newman for putting this collection out there and its cool cover; to Rupert Loydell for his so many years of supporting my writing as well as contribution to this book's cover, and to Jackie Moore for her thoughtfulness about, encouragement of and insights on my writing journey to the here and now.

Supported using public funding by

**ARTS COUNCIL
ENGLAND**

LOTTERY FUNDED

Contents

THE LONESOMEST SOUND

When Searching

An attempt to find something is a pursuit or a hunt but discovery will be differentiated. Turning an eye to the sound of a plane is a deception. Looking under rocks and other allusions. After an inappropriate amount of time he will find something suitable to wear at that wedding. There are directions and there is being directed. A horizon is a romantic vista for searching. It is even a quest though this has all the makings of a pretence. To iterate it is to make a kenning of action but never the intent. Find things, find love, find happiness, find peace. They are all in the wardrobe. Keep advancing the pages. To be reliant on the acquisition is to close all of the doors.

Finding Nothing

It is hardly existential. This glass with traces of damp becoming ecstasy. Witness of a means to an end. Rolling rocks over and over until they gather a morsel of more than the nothing left behind. Hour after hour, fishermen do it with all kinds of tackle. How to expatriate the nil of love believing a home is somewhere waiting. Is an emerald really ever more than its colour? There is no hopeful proverb in the discovery of absence. You enter the room as before and once upon the window, pull open these curtains to look outside and continue. It will come of it. The calm of knowing if you actually found some, chaos would destroy a whole night. She just laughed, and that is enough.

UFO

Unless actually found they're obfuscation. And now for the real deal: Space Force Regulation 200-2. A glow of aura and awe and the auspicious in a sighting. When conspiracy is so much closer to home. Would we go if asked, promised no answers but more wondrous mysteries than could be dreamt of defining? Belief in a magic three – UFO or GOD, the extra-terrestrial versus the celestial, always somewhere other and beyond. The mistake is in its *flying*, as if this is the only alien methodology of arrival. Spruce budworms and thunderstorms debunk the nocturnal seeing into illusion.

Coast

They tried to rescue the sun but it was rising and disappearing in its haze. A fisherman's big voice carries like the squeal of a seagull. On water, light remained. Depositional features subside with the ebb. Amalgamated by distance, clouds lowered to darkness. Horses ridden on the sand sink to their stomachs but still have nothing to say. Real waves seemed like the difference in black and white. Haar and fret romanticise droplets of water. There will be a purpose somewhere further along.

Confession

Catharsis and storm drain. How the wave of a hand absolves and awaits the next gesture. To seek forgiveness from the wronged in their abject destruction at *your* hands. Penance so swift and immediate, it ought to rank with the sub four-minute mile. Intention is everything. That ol' prodigal fallacy again. The Healing of the Sealing. Sacrament from the return of a long and loved debauchery. Sin's. Judge and jury through the conduit from a garment to a believing. A Roman Catholic App. Tell Her what you did #MeToo. If the first is true and the second a lie, where does the third sit on the Arc of Reconciliation?

Waiting a Long Time

In case a certain little lady walks by. Time passes on a high in a citadel. Fulfilment is not it having reached the brim. And then two holy ghosts come along. When reaching that buttress reveals the next one. If it is the status quo you will know what is coming. The franchises for hanging around were sold out long ago, ironically. All those who have joined the queue to tell their stories of standing around. When the rain came it hadn't changed.

The Speed of Death

It is a steady wave the same as a calm sea but one way. Thirty micrometres a minute; two millimetres an hour: I think that is pedestrian in the great scheme of things. And if they are taking this long, where will they go? Other studies – less precise – work it out for hangings. Oracle of the cytoplasm and green globs. I don't know if I am angry or saddened when she tells me of her waiting. Apoptosis of this mortal coil. How science strips the Grim Reaper of its robes. Population dynamics and population genetics: go figure. The death of speed of light decay has its own abstract so there are other darknesses explored beyond our comprehension.

In the Palm of a Hand

An unlikely place for the inscription of control. Where mercy has life lines. Red spots and peeling skin are beyond yours. It does not mean that one when saying you must choose the right hand to read. The irony there is so much on pain. Fawning like a caress. Knowing there rather than the back is to hold all the secrets and subterfuge. Idiomatic of the inner part, unless a supplicant.

The Philosophy of Being
Delayed on a Train

A tannoy does not express a doctrine. Delays are explained – in documentation – through the calm rhetoric of platitude and irony. That Dialectical Theory of Staggered Time is considered a load of bollocks by passengers. *The train got delayed* presupposes a self-sense of desire and/or expectation. An epistemic utility of knowing the amount of time in its procrastination rather than a happening itself. How Bertrand Russell got delayed before getting on his at the Gare du Nord. Simultaneity of timetable / leaving / track / leaves. For me, our tolerance for or sensitivity to delay exists as variables in an expression that looks impenetrably like mathematics. Dickens' mimetic capture was of the unstoppable forward thrust into death.

Algorithms

Processing blind data for a perfect night put. Going back, time-travel is coded in vowels and consonants. An emoji added to giggle solutions. Self-driving over a cliff in technical despair. Elucidation of selves in unambiguous diatribes / angst in the existential poetry of numbers calculated as soliloquy. Where functionality is massaged by control. Intimate questions asked from scans of average affections. How procedure terminates at the first and foremost result. One step beyond and it's curtains. When that love of language becomes a *longform* communication. Emergence of computational self-harm.

In an Arid Desert

Barren and hostile and so full of potential. You don't need a Crane to lift a bitter grain of sand, though catching on the wind requires another poetry. Its parched yet surviving history. Where the latitudes embrace a heat of extraordinary sameness. Night's minute exchanges from the epidermis of leaves. Plant alphabet: agaves / brittlebush / ephedras / false mesquite / ocotillo / sotol / yuccas. Animal alphabet: burrowers and other secreted rats. A horse with no name introduced me to her on that hot night. This physiological adaptation in a realm of niche and the ephemeral. Precipitate on a perception of water. Uplift beats erosion like a full house this four-of-a-kind.

Electracy

Knowing a keyboard like the back of a digital strand. With this instant speed we were there just before the catastrophe. Dearest prudence. In the blink of an AI. Anticipating the grammatology of a future shift, when Derrida lectured in French I thought it was his speaking that clouded my understanding. In the now time of accidental disaster we are plugged into its circuitry. How the Rhetoric of Digits is not a gesture from the hand. Participatory practices may require wind and sun and waves when the other powers are cut. I have escaped that theatre to regain control over sum of these words.

Internalised

I do not think the demons honour humility. If fluidity cannot find an outlet it will flow around and around inside. Passion in its own latitudes of forever. In the desert places of frost. Medicine best kept internal will work only on the arid habitats of brooding, though never cure. In this heated introspection it is the ironic undertow of an iceberg. When poetry is parched to describe but speaks from within by reading between the lines. If the sacred is never external the struggle to survive is irrelevant. Solipsism can crawl around inside any dry and roughened terrain. Considering outlines on the dunes of our subconscious, their formation contours to both good and bad meditation.

Moon Behind Pampas Grass

Caesar's horse impressed by the surprise of such a film existing. Swingers meet by its light, apparently. Luna 'n' cortaderia selloana. In the metaphysics of a photograph, dark lines are drawn against the brightness of illumination. Animal motifs should not be sketched from strands and luminosity. Emblem of autumn and replanting. Cartoon versions present displays of singular leaves. Simon's chainsaw another exercise in hacking away at metaphors. I could count the number of my moon pics on many hands. Beware of the pink, but not because of any sexual allure.

Posthumanism

In the sonnet of this future there are at least 2 x 7 definitions of our demise in the yin yang of hanging on. Epistemologically speaking, the terminology *will be back*. Despite my confirmation in Dreifaltigkeitskirche Worms, what I do understand is how at our core there is still no God. It will be the most existential surge protection. When we are all members of The Agency, at what point is being enmeshed our evolution? Beckett has already given a voice to the physically disconnected mouth. And I have no more human words for this triumvirate of beginnings.

Word Sin

It is possible to transgress beyond parameters set for yourself, like not mentioning a pronoun removed from this. The evil mischief of autocorrect. *In the beginning* was not the original, perhaps. Corrupting a rhyming couplet with dissonance, and only for effect. He was sat; it was slippy. The only opposite is to say you didn't write it. In the RhymeChest of *sin* there is *spin* and that is contemporary sacrilege. When it is stripped right back to the bare bones of cleverness. For dearth/greed/indifference/fakery of another word. Most of my caring life has been to use them without guilt or fear.

No Blood Moon

There is no apocalypse when dark clouds roll in all evening. Other moons photographed through the fingers of a tree's branch always deliver their narratives. To be under the impression of an umbra. But there were black tufts of filled sackcloth in the sky. Looking closer for failure, it is years since the escallonia bloomed. Mars too bowing behind drawn curtains. My intuition pierced, it wasn't by light, red or bright, and karma was never going to be found in rain killing this heat wave the following day. Still a minion of the sun.

Purple Turbines

First it is insects, then bats are eviscerated. Hearing they could be painted another colour, he was *blown away*. The transparency of air churned without censure or colour-coding. Ugly things in the beauty of function and relativity. Normally white yet not even for that hint of happiness. What becomes of the purple sandpiper? A blade of anisotropic eroticism in some whirls. A giraffe's tongue deters sunburn and the flittermouse.

There's Always Grammar

You can say it is much better if it makes you feel – filler – better. There are those who say you should never begin a sentence with *there is/are* and there is a sense of terrorism in this. Play it again Gram. How mentioning the word *poetry* breaks convention. None of all this matters. How the fuck is *there is happiness* not making sense as an expletive sentence? Prime and Target do not run together like *leaf* and *death* though assonance makes sense of sound too. The Dialect of Liberation.

Taking the Easiest Route

Wolves became dogs to live on it. When a man from Minneapolis wants a line on the easiest route to Wichita. Water knows. Sheep carve diagonals where steep. People defer to signs or write poems, one or the other. The bees dance all day on lavender planted for them, purple springing upwards each time they leap. How would you know until you had sampled the alternative? I take the simplest course, therefore I am. Like a Sunday morning. We noticed this late afternoon how our tall false acacia leans all one way.

Wind-Powered Sun

So what came first, the sun or the wind or the word *solar?*
Conversion is the link in interdependence. Off-grid, wind
wanders where the sun does not shine. Hybrids take Nature
to new highs in inbreeding. Ships which sailed the Nile were
powered more by prophecy than moving air. Downdrafts that
churn are energy hallucinations of sunshine burns. King Lear
in his madness cracked open the moulds to new technologies.
Uneven heat on roughness and rotation blows and blows and
blows. An Aeolian harp shines too / meets gods above hills where
sound is light powered by the wind.

Thicker Than Rain-drops on November Thorn

And so we must ask, *what is?* I can imagine many things, but for Samuel it might well be Misery. Where is Agatha Christie when needed? Blood. An obvious would be rime, but I like the idea of frosted thoughts. In years to come, the hydrophobic thorn will bounce the rain away. There are those who would sanitise with Melancholy. Baigent paints a brooding answer with piano twirls. It is just fragmentary. To break up the 'chubby symmetry' is not a metaphor Coleridge would use, as much as he loved perfections in nature.

Balloons and Criminals

A view from above in the drifting silence of intrusion. It is an inflation of desire that leads to wrongdoing. Filling with helium and poetry attached, one drifted to an open prison: its poem on captive animals. Thieves laugh and think it is all a gas. Condemned to death, felons piloted yet never found freedom in their heated air. Innocence is never so bulbous. The irony of Francois' rise and fall. When you hold on, climbing, and the thing you stole is retribution.

Prodigal Son

Never returning home, and with those many times in a pigsty all that enlightened was leaving again. You can love whoever for whatever without the need for narrative. Placing a parable in a colloquial aside is like painting with sand. Our sly cries and raw provocations. A return to form can mean how prose replaces the sonnet. A restoration of the sun beyond a horizon of tall trees. Of course, he did not literally return to a place that never existed. Redemption in shame, apparently. I turned away, many years ago, and these are the consequences of having been there in the first place.

Moss Undulations

The *motion of waves* is prettier than *corrugated*. This continuous up and down of heavy breathing. A curling of growing. These belong to humans – a roof draped over a secret. Even in its natural morphology there would be no ebb and flow of colour. Snaking. But I don't want a solution. Verdant ripples modulating. A physical basis for fascination. If you could smoke it, imagine the gentle turbulence of your feelings. This mole once drew similar lines across the lawn but had no idea about patterning. Plasma membrane types do it all for the pollen walls. And top dressings would smooth out any inherent aversions.

About Writing Poetry

Avoid sentimentality unless it prompts laughter. Shakespeare died to save you from trying to write like him. The stress is there to make the mood and line. When they say *let your subject find you* there is a deep sense of loss. The *5 Ways*, the *7 Ingredients*, the *9 Steps* and the *13 Tips* – when advice in odd numbers is marginally more assuring than that given. Coleridge said it best. I like the idea of a dumb, silent poem being. I have suddenly / as if urge is all one needs / written this form here. All my sonnets are about themselves because they are defined. Poetry that fails when a pig eats the bacon of its rhyme. You want purpose?

A Good Life

Golden rules are ten for nothing on the internet. When you have a lot but need a little or when you have little and fully accept this is your lot. Then there is the one about the glass. There are also six other rules, first-rate too, and five secrets. Aristotle had eleven. Mark Twain had nine. Being a maths teacher is having a head start. Growing you own number of ideas for the self-sufficiency of goodness. The holistic is fashionable. Find love, find happiness, find peace, find shame. Gold. Buy the membership. Speak a few reasonable words, and in any language. Ne'er tarry. Get a membership discount. There are estate agents who make promises. That we have a coherent narrative, even when listening to spiritual music.

When You Have a Disability

So I wrap her tightly in a cocoon of protection, letting in air and sunlight and food and love and a finite distance to walk and precious sleep if and when and the miserable truth of a rationale that it could be worse. There are others: disinclination / distancing / disliking. And they have rights, just not those. References are so drearily pragmatic. It is forty years and the strength is remarkable for someone who apparently has less than others. In efforts to define I found this one of the least understandable – *describing a disability does not make a disability*. There are more: disclosure / disinformation / disbelief. Of course, misreading is not an impairment but I found this momentarily salient – *text anxiety is not considered a disability*. Sometimes you have to laugh.

Being Death

You are proud and mightily so. After all these years and that act of faith in your defiance. Priests speaking at funerals offer different promises. Beckett's *lessness* or *habit* – this is no quandary you'll have the time or need to ponder. Never the spectator. Making it sweet is the same nothing of hope. I've seen enough of what it was for now. Stream of afterlife. Last wishes are the generous promise of no looking back. Dasein sucking the life out of himself. What if it isn't as bad as we think? The clumsy portmanteau of *being-unto-death*. This vexed question of a night-owl hooting itself to extinction.

Inside Out

When you leave empty-handed filled to capaciousness. It must
be love. A playful paradox for the masses. Out there will always
be so much further away than in here. The participatory of its
invitation leaves too many standing at the doorway. Hospitality
in transition. It is so farfetched people have been running
after all day and night. There will always be an opportunity to
misunderstand the other way around. Can you imagine scientists
ruining this mystery? Bring a rug to sit on its lawn and feel a part
of the experiment. Fake views. Like a knot tied within the most
basic of parameters.

The Nature of Artifice

This, naturally. When synthetic stimuli is in ascendance. Art that's read in truth and awe. We scrutinise ingredients, cautious of the sleight and ruse, hungry for what fills but also keeps us well. Quintessence of fake news. The species and the sex #MeToo. *Nor sophisticated by art* as we live now in a world where boundaries compose to merge but are also pushed miles apart. When Trump reads Aristotle. *V* we have sheared from the hedge for her name and verisimilitude. These tales you continue to tell and their remove from moments of experience. Photoshop. Where the landscape no longer has its horizon.

Redemption

It is crushing as religious trope / it is hope in the simplicity of honest regret. Salvage. Considering the cost, to retune my turbo is easier than atoning for those mistakes. How this gig economy is the major deliverance of what we redeem. Recovery. Marley's *forward to this generation.* An eye for an eye and looking deep into one another's gaze with the follow-on of bites. When the righteous suit is granted. Rather than have it here on earth, we are obliged to proclaim to others for reward's afterthought. Writing about it enough with these secular anchors, trusting the truth of always having tried.

Firing Squad

The concept is simple. Dostoevsky tells a convincing scenario or two. Teach students ardent for figurative accuracy how *rat-a-tat-tat* is not always onomatopoeic, nor *fusillading* a euphemism. A disarray in the round. When we ask *is a firing squad more humane than lethal injection?* Art in the symmetry of position and sound. When the sentenceé is seated only seven shooters needs be stationed for the silencing. But teach them the deep irony and punning of *unconstitutional pain*. And as we are exploring language and meaning, there is the Boy Scouts' *Firing Squad Skit* ...

Gristle on the Bolted Kitchen Door

The sinew of indigestible gestures in love. Out of your blues. If you gather around there will be dropped crumbs of secret thoughts. Haunches leap inside themselves with their elastin. Where the rods on back door and front gate have some sense of equilibrium in staying drawn. Knives and forks set from outward to in is as pretentious as that surface of glass. If chewing too hard you might get symptoms before synonyms. Fasteners that do not run as quickly as him. When bespoken they converse by individual tongue and groove. Posing in the throb of that body's journey. App-enabled for playfulness. Strangers are not allowed to work at the informality of its furniture.

Preserving Pears

There are my vigilante moves in the early morning. Can I just use bourbon? Raiding a *friend's* tree is some kind of irony. Too many YouTube recipes eschewing sugar. A 15-carbon skeleton at its core, fleshed out until disintegration / unless. When I come to check for falls, is it possible they hear me walking on gravel? Worms and birds have their own ideas. Phrenology of a fruit anticipating its longevity. She adorned with small squares of cheese, knowing and tempting. It is in the merest hint of self-sufficiency. Both the pear and the plum trees have become sustainable sonnets. As if a loanword can preserve its naming.

The Nature of Dialogue

I always refused to apply pragmatics to Shakespeare's. It's all just talk talk talk. In its birthday suit, what is said by consenting speakers continually sounds unadorned. Her backchanneling goes viral in a crowd. The best we can be is listeners. I would always prefer to hear Carver hearing others when representing the interchanges of speech. Oracy in the classroom – that natural dynamics of learning when they talk to one another, igniting. Tentative in nature / touching certainty in conversation. *like like like like like like like like like like* in iambic pentameter is still a filler.

Tarrying

Where the Holy Ghost is like a bus. I imagine leaning on anything is best. Having the time to stop and stare rather than delay. When waiting for the meeting is a tautology. There are sixty four instances in the bible. Gathering rosebuds could usurp leaning if one felt the need for positivity. Not that I understand, obviously, but I like the idea that this is temporal and therefore possible for all of us. In case a certain little lady comes by. Then there is the sub four-minute tarry that broke all the rules. Abiding with procrastination? In the Book of Revelations – unlike Matthew, Mark, Luke and John – there are four times all exactly the same and we do not have to believe in any of them.

Law of Diminishing Returns

In the pat-on-the-back of wishful thinking, it is one that can be broken. Secondary progressive. The pumpkin farmer has to think carefully before investing in extra orange-making, especially on the other side of October's end. Perspective would plausibly view it as an illusion yet never gets near enough to judge for sure. Wellbeing too muses on the input/output model of bigger smiling when the face begins to hurt. The marathon runner's wall. Crop models that yield to psychological considerations. When a theory determines *at a specific point* is it not also theoretically possible to digress and create distance? Mathematics in this are marginal. There are multiple ways to lessen.

Whiskers in the Sink

Like looking at starling murmurations. Lint roller and masking tape are serious if sad suggestions for the clean-up. The Bear Family shave alfresco. How even these fall and are written into polished contours of a sermon. If not *manly*, have we all moved on? Assume love. A TripAdvisor share. That plumber's guide not mentioning baking soda and white vinegar and other home truths. E / A / D / A played on guitar or ukulele or piano. *Cheap canned goop works a treat,* according to porcelain preachers. Gomer and Dittmar and Neuman postulate on diffusing tips from whisker sides. Beard Care Catcher Apron can be found cheaply on eBay. Whisker-evoked responses are a revelation. There are generic groom catchers too, by the way.

Not Writing About a Skein Arrowing Through the Sky

This isn't a tale and I do not mean the yarn. How each typed command is a knot, so another metaphor for avoidance. It will not be so much the cliché as the verb, though I do not feel it is as diabolical as a *shard*. For all of the writerly deflection, watching still draws out a sense of ending. Weavers might form it? Back to the righteous ignoring, there comes a point – no pun intended, obviously – when reliance on the precursor usurps anxiety. On second thoughts, the weavers' art is a misreading. Loose composition breaks formation. The September skyline was grey and they a line of black in an ordinary shape.

The Nature of Interpretation

We see most signing on our TVs at storm warnings and mass shootings. If I cannot hear your tone I have little understanding of how much you like or dislike this listening. How ironic to be concerned by construal in qualitative research. There is less in science, but who really wants to experience beyond hypothesis? For example, her relationship with nature is all about that first touch and taking home what's found to put away forever in sealed storage. It is an adaptation to realities. Terrains navigable because of their interpretative plotting of where it is safe to intrude poetically. That jury who hold it all in their hands. In deciding, we reach at length and that is such a stretch.

Dementia's Mantra

Where am I? Forgetfulness is no excuse for being ignored by the thoughtless. Their rise and fall. *Why am I here?* Mood is / behaviour is / bright was / calm was. Where confusion is worse than loss. *When can I come home?* They are not dead, you know, but are somewhere else where it isn't measured as it used to be. And depression. *Where am I?* To reach this stage you wouldn't have thought there were others. Adventure though the connection with what is occasionally recalled. *Why am I here?* Anatomically annotated, the colours will not be remembered for their appropriateness. Prosaic targets for neurodegeneration. *When can I come home?*

Night's Lighted Garden

It is only ornamental if you have exchanged money. Lit like an argument between two verbs. The wildlife can close their eyes with the rest of us. When a waxing crescent is in that position it will be captured and transitioned to its other illuminations. Enchanted by technology / as decorative as nature allows. Imagine just having to look and remember. Such a long way from its noise in Ted's bucket. Each night by this moon my discarded solar light is motioned on until it dies. Rhapsody of enhancement. Where word-use is over two hundred years old, the moon's is significantly more.

Significant Rain Effect

Lazy or euphemism or no experience of death and destruction. To precipitate in its downfall. How mountains squeeze out the inequalities, wanting it or not. So much more than a watery affectation. Being followed by a rain shadow. That year El Niño lost its mystique. A sensitivity analysis can weep in symbiosis. You can be well prepared if you turn around and do not drown. After she pulled out the plant dry as tumbleweed, even after those many storms. Stalled in the car when my students jumped into that flooded ford and pushed me all the way through. A phrenology of plants that think about their drowning.

Language on the Outside

As if we didn't think it first. Forward-channelling for continuance. In the learning destination of heat rising and other auras. Differences between form and meaning would get a better airing there, breathing noticed too. You see, the outside-in / inside-out dichotomy has application beyond the discussions of contrariness. According to Wittgenstein, it is easier to hold one's tongue from this position. In the all-around and everywhere external, babel we will only hear and never have to indulge in speaking. Sentences can be processed outside the focus of attention and this is what we call poetry.

Fallen Trees

To make a clearing there will sometimes be this intentional legacy. They can stumble too. What makes this so different to autumn leaves? Many can be righted, unlike those who had been set in their ways. Pool-riffles repeat rhythms of stairstep streams that undermine. Their habitat value is calculated in the years of being left alone. This kind of healing is the essence of altruism. Storm inventories will name numbers over species. Windthrown, distances travelled are usually small. Time and space and direction of fall form a myriad of tree-contemplation. Seen and unseen, all decay eventually makes its terrestrial bed. Those that make it to the sea deprive soil of what perpetrates journeying. Deadwood in the Otherworld is not a game.

Renaissance

If it is repeating, that is just the same and this is not good enough. Making new is the oldest lie. An annual pass is a shortcut halfway up the mountain. Restitution obliges something better than belief. Q&A: what is renewal these days? / the tabula rasa of necessity. If you pack everything up in boxes without labels, the existential will organise its own repositioning. When done tacitly you cannot hear each other's despair. E-renewal takes the fun out of that face-to-face challenge for more. *This due for renew* is the first line of your rhyme-heavy haiku. When vows seem to need this, it is time to be unavowed. The yang of cancellation is surely apocalyptic.

Word Wall

You'll see: saviours and monsters aren't and are. The street is a home and not a house. To word a lie these days is less than a falsehood / which is itself no more than a slip of the tongue / that could be construed as a nuance / for which no apology is required. But the art critic who could not say *far out*. Using un in a ravel sentence. To semanticise her lover of language with a branch. Pleonasm stopped. Communication breakdown: give up / surrender; leave out / omit; hold up / delay; turn down / reject; pass out / comatose. How millennials woke to the change of meaning in their lives. The annoying anaphora of babel. Let's call it symmetry – Beowulf has no plæse here; Grendel sy.

Domination

Imagine if it wasn't to do with power at all. Where this incorporates modifiers as if less of the sway will assuage. Control with knobs on. How a root like *dominus* is steeped in knowing subjugation. Humiliation is more than enough. As absolutes go, this is this. In the expansive game of reality, players who hide behind are at the forefront of a worldwide. When its number is $y (G)$ we are already under the spell by our incomprehension. Ozymandias was not someone to ultimately ask. The Anarchist Archives is home to many relevant resources. When flying its colours we'd prefer not to believe them. Some call it a dark history and now we have posthumanism. Politics against are bathed in such innocence we savour the calmest hope good ignorance can offer.

Finding Objects & Artifacts

Although it can be digitized, we still need tools for digging and the will to invade and intrude. When people had ideas for the pragmatic, it never occurred there would be this meaninglessness when aesthetes found everything out of time and place. Early words the sound of thinking about a future. Gender and intimacy in the curve of carving and seeming softness of cloth. When speaking for its creator, at least there is this feel for a finality of death. *Ephemera* wraps the palpable in its own genuine sense of once upon. Fetching fetishisms. Ontology of ovals and other wheels. I understand the discovery and learning, but when they had no concept of precursors and anxiety. Object culture objectified. The primacy of their own sauciness and savouring. Given shape by humans in ignorance and incipience. And if we treated them all the same? This absolute essence of the found.

Lazarus

What is it with Luke and John and their competing optimisms? That multi-media pervasiveness. Furniture restoration lays down a marker in its lifting to a terrestrial pristine. There is *Powerheart G3 Pro, Lifeline, Defibtech, HeartSine samaritan 360p*, but a missed trick in the absence of *Lazarus Original*. When the pampas stems returned after all those years. Imagine the multitude of lazaruses from plague and war that aren't zombiefied. This 'straightening from under again' transcends as a more telluric phrase. How we salve disappointment in mocking the grandiloquence of redemption. In searching for a pun, there is 'raising hell' and then the corrective of *'raisin bread'*.

Wild Imagination

She says the most extraordinary, unbelievable things, and knows she's not thinking but believes that this is the truth. It is the creative gene and ghosts that walk the corridors of her home at night brush past and are cold to the definite touch. Imagine sitting on a sofa in a room surrounded by people listening wide-eyed and also having faith and she tells them as if everything is more real than even that. Credibility. Poets have it and can make theirs sound so wonderful / priests have incantation and incense and other accoutrements yet the years of abuse are unravelling in the aisles. If only the honesty of prose could be so lavish and persuasive. It is because she was regaling with this kind of wild recall and someone looked on with a slight but knowing grin.

Influence of Anxiety

How a search engine rejects the inversion, anxious of getting it wrong. In a testing regime there are those who will be destroyed. If performance modulates perception I worry how I must write this better than before. When she suggested there was no stress, others felt this room withering. Their *drive increment* drives me crazy. Movement and grace mediated across its divide like bending a bamboo cane into the fallen corn. How threatening stimuli processes itself without beck and call. I know about it from her and through me, resisting both but needing their instruction.

Conversions

Weights and measures are easiest, but try emotion beyond the simplicities of yin yang. Talking dirty about love is not all that far along the scale. When there is nothing left to subtract, nothing can be taken back. The logic of it optimises hope. All those bright lights and trumpets blaring and you find yourself having wandered into a neighbour's alfresco party. There is probability in any shift. In considering arithmetic a hoot there is a sense that someone has made it to the very end. Oddly, Confirmation is far less binding over time.

Flippancy

Those who are pranksters rather than wits. There is a false freedom in avoiding the other kind of thought. Imagine a war started because of it. Elliptically speaking, there is no argument. The poetics of flippancy finds meaning somewhere within a narrative of itself. Fundamentally, despite armed citizens being glib, gunshots will kill in an ass kicking. When you look in the mirror are you always laughing? The joke made, it is for others to decide if it was. But what a gesture. Knitting an argument in its lattice of facetiousness. Wanting thanksgiving is completely naïve.

Meaning

In the sarcasm of its question. As / Bec / kett / would / say / in / his / I / rish / lilt: *think about rhythm.* As Jim would say: *break on through (to the other side).* If each thing is a living speaking godthing unfolding, the words of this are going to be more convoluted than we could have imagined. The dictionary is certainly at one end. Inscribed on the badges philosophers hand out after your first cleared hurdle. But if language is always shifting so too is this. Looking for happiness is meaningless if never found, apparently. Semiotics of signage as it is thought but never seen. *The meaning of meaning* is a more scholarly search. Where dogmas collide.

Tangibility

The *almost* of touch is as deceptive as definition. Dozier has assured he will be there for the feeling. Perhaps imaginable in your dreams when hitting the ground so hard. These tangible synonyms are often as heavy as nothingness. If seeing was enough there would be no need for this caress or even punch in my gut. Ancient aliens with *tangibilis* tattooed on their array of appendages. Bertrand Russell has a query about the discernibility proffered by any sense. Those intangible assets of evil. An impact of now rather than what we think it might mean in years fallen away. As an abstract, the theory of touching is tender. Datum doubts. *Solutions* and *Results* that trip off the palpable tongue. Virtual tangibility still requires the wearing of gloves.

I Guess Jesus on the Cross Can be Found in Most Churches

Some kids never leave home. Précised to a *crucifix* it is no less prominent. Representation of the instrument of passing the buck. Fragments of truth are said to be here and there but you'd have to have faith to fall for that one. Those Protestants! This Lutheran! A last visit to church to celebrate Coleridge blaspheming *a light in sound, a sound-like power in light*. Listen Billy, if god looks at us like a jeweller at a diamond, isn't there sparkle enough, whatever the defects, to dispense with redemption? An old man lying dead and prostrate in the garden he loved, both shoulders touching a long piece of wood across his back. Samuel later deferred to orthodoxy.

The Lonesomest Sound

Naturally a superlative inhabited by pedal steel and whippoorwill. There is the freight train too, but only from a romantic distance. It is universal when you hear it anywhere. Woody's curfew blues when the wind blows awry. There is the turn of a key, yet which way? Field recordings of absence. Found in the whole of Huck's narrative where the wail is everything just before that thought of death. Other cultures will sing this lament but eschew the banjo. Ray's pancakes are incongruent, despite his plaintive *lonesomest lonesome*. The keeper's gibbet is a lesser and more visual thing. It may be possible this cannot be programed. Is it Doppler more than the mode of transport?

Someone is Watching the Narrative

If narrative constructs and someone is watching, there is a realm of reading that sees. The first person is privileged numerically. They say it is a science of the sensory cortex which feels creativity. Outcomes are as far as the lines can be. The story within the story as observed of a writer pouring words into our ears. Revisits enlighten as much as they obscure, but only if you were never there. Chronicles of death present theories we await in an allotted time to validate. Tap and hold a story if it must be screened for viewing / turn off in the transition of your believing. At the end, someone wrote it all as procedural and we too watched as well as followed.

All Bodies

There is free delivery on eligible orders, cadavers or living, but exact mass is required. The educational value of exhibiting yours goes beyond self-gratification. To explore deep within the human body, close your eyes having first bound tight the hands. Perfectly preserved, these are their deaths. Behind the seams the better materials of lace and mesh and velvet are growing. A circus for every shape and size, the tent is being erected by the river as I write this review. The leotard speaks for truth. Positive stories are like fables of hope. The umbrella and the crown and the shroud: these are the layers of varying concealment. Exhumed in the interests of overcoming ennui. Bionic but unruly, there is always a price to pay for creation.

Not Amused

Where *we* is a pronoun but irrelevant. If you ain't done nothing you ain't likely to be annoyed. On a rainy afternoon and there are no jokes in the dark clouds. Not absurd enough even when sung by the tenor of a laughing angel. Meme is a meme is a meme is a meme. A range of conversational data cannot pinpoint all moments. Avatar without a smile in its programming. Heretical humour gathers dust on the shirtsleeves of sulking clowns. When teachers are not amused I do not think real learning can take place. It is universal, and there are translations, but that would be cheating. If there was an anthem would it be sung through gritted teeth? It is the odd negative.

Found in Writing

Love letter in a bottle, as dry as this arrival on sand and its antiquity in speaking of possession. Cave poems as near to concrete writing as real stone allows. How sonnets are always fourteen lines but anything otherwise, unless about war. Turning Folio pages by gloveless hands was the commodity fetish of a lifetime. Baudelaire's prose poems in translation are still a prostitution of these and his other artifices. How reading between the lines is what it's all about. Counting ways the literacy of electracy is more than a disappearance of words. Would Thomas / Hood bother to / rhyme first words every / time or / is / this literary myth? My still boxed Parker pen on its ruby wedding anniversary. When finding those teenage Romantic poems, I wish I'd howled instead. American cursive in my mother's letters will always remind how close we were in writing across miles and time and belonging.

Trim Tab

And the people's revolution. Small fry to the big fry like simile to the metaphor. So that it has positive sway but not a populism which crashes the aerodynamics learned from history. Schumacher size / secondary to the primary rudder. As if people mattered. Articulating up and down on the plane of an argument otherwise going to hell. Its promise to the Angel of Death is a smooth ride on the long drive up the cemetery path. Using sensors to automate the correction of leanings to wrong ways. *Aileron* for extra finesse. Even eBay sells their panacea. Pneumatic ballet on a stage more ancient than that first comedy of dance.

Job

Not that, but the one about a slave to suffering and fantasy. Transcends one religion to the next conscription. It is a story I disdain with all my will and yet live every day. Them and Uz. Even the chiming minstrels Termanite, Shushite & Naamathite failed to assuage pain through rhyme. A thumb-screw of mythology. Had Satan considered tender torture, tempting with paradox? Where reward is excess and pain: ten more needy kids; all those stinking camels! The woman was a wife and endured too.

Expectancy

New life in a new coil spring. Statistical probability for longevity does not appear to have a logarithm for accidents. You see it in the large wide white of eyes, both ways. It is only everything when absolutely nothing else transpires. Motivation in the selection of behaviour itself self-selecting. Imagine the middle name *Valence*. That difference of 3.8 years could link to a poem about isolation and loneliness. When minding the growing gap, beware a dangerous leap of anticipation. *Dead at Whenever* is a study compiled by indifference. You would think someone called Victor Vroom would have a turbo theory of life expectancy.

Looking Into the Doorway

She almost held her hand walking to that place and both looked with the indifference of having a job to do. There is an argument that most will gaze through rather than into. Being framed within forgetfulness. Peephole on a larger scale. You imagine there is a future in every passing. Romanticism paints a garden with fruit and stone walls covered in vines and perhaps a view of the sea beyond and the kind of transition to which they must never close their eyes. Maturity is no guarantee of returning. Asking about what's behind is a quite different genre. Don't be inane: only time travels through itself. As portals go, these smack of the mundane.

Now I Lay Me Down to Sleep

A child's prayer with all the adult insistence of ritual. *Foshadi:* in Latin etymology, its esoterica is hard to find. Could this explain the pains in my knees after all these years? For the Sylhetis it means *troublesome,* and that was the response in my eventual apocalypse. The power of rhyme when words are irrelevant. *Foshadi:* a near firecracker of an illusion. If you search long and deep enough there will be places to visit, things to buy and other mantras to learn by heart. In the actual line, its paradox is both wonderful and frightening. *Foshadi:* my first fake news, by more ways than one. And had I ever, where would mishearing and misknowing have taken me in that death?

In the Basement

Remembered hearing The Supremes on a windowsill radio, secretly changing to cool shoes for school. There are example sentences for use of the subject word. Horrors hidden across the culture of abuse. Moisture. Chameleon no longer changing in its jar. Reciting a poem in one, days before leaving forever. At Uncle Glenn's with those magazines. There are refurbishments but the view from a ground-level window remains subliminal. Testing a cat's landing from the height of a roaring furnace. Recurring dream of how it moves from one opening space to another, always bending darkness into light. Imagined it safer than assuming the nuclear position beneath a desk. Where poets write in damp and bones. The mild beatings I endured.

There is No Such Thing as Nothing

I could understand the cosmic search, yet it is overly obvious as the initial port. The Fugs proving otherwise. It will always be the deepest irony when pursuing. Leering at it all day to try and see. Where there is some probability. Aristotle again put his finger in and on to prove by more ways than one. As we can contemplate it. How I would explore the discourse all night when drugs and Monopoly no longer engaged. It is all bubbles and foam. As for Absolute Nothing, it is more about semantics than shrinkage as poets play its game with a wasted deck of cards.

Stories and Lies

Those we tell ourselves and then those we tell ourselves again. The good and the juicier. In a complex world, either can get lost after their renditions. *You light my fire* is one from each domain. The Seven Deadly Spins. A science of deception is learned by sleeping outside. The ghost of the one which was your least impressive. Why art thrives. Imagine how refugees suffer these narratives. I say, the art of it. Prospero or Gatsby? You learn the nine clues to detect a lie then find an oracle with ten: is this one extra or ten different? Artifice of a narcissist. The bathos of fake news.

An Inventory of Loss

If it isn't in the customers' hands there might be some institutional pilfering. All those ships that sailed to the wrong destinations. A perpetual system would sadly prevent learning from deprivation. Obsolescence is not disappearance so the heart will ache all the same. Write-offs at the corral of just about acceptable. Put the fraudulent into perspective – there is still a something to hold and endear and fulfil. At night I rearrange everything on the table by moving into impeccable angles in the centre and perfect placements at corners until still seeing the mess she must never lose making if I am to survive. A fire sweeping through is for a moment's familiar touch.

Credentials

De facto authorisation to pocket as much suggestion of belonging you think you alone can blag. Proof in a tenuous world casting immediate doubt. Card-carrying competency in alliteration. Certificates on the wall / lined along the hall / no award for the existential fall. Nodes as nods to endorsement. Show at a door before they will open – here is the threshold craved and allowed and disappointing when rolled into one overconfident step. Card-carrying fraudster of fake wares. Mine lifts a barrier to that long grandiose drive around the bend.

You Cannot Live on Beauty Alone

Because what you hear as the sound of children playing is just the calls of seabirds. A home resurrected after drought and lowered waters is still a relic. Romanticism was a power of light until Sara intruded with her orthodox diss. Beauty in loneliness can be self-indulgent. As Monroe purred, *a career is wonderful, but you can't curl up with it on a cold night.* I think Curley's wife too knew a dress and sunlight was never enough. Sustenance groomed is still potatoes. Has anyone mentioned the folly of this?

Autumn in its Water

In another part of the world – which I know well – it will be the fall into a river. To see this as a distortion caused by ripples is denying *differance*. Colours are the same, if in other places. Maintenance of a pond tends to consider shades of blue and green and those darknesses as intrusions rather than art. The element of water is mutable / what does not is not real, though this will be in any season. An autumnal beach carries stones applauding to the shore as before. Concentric curves act like gel in the amalgamating. When hearing the phrase *trees are dressed* you go back and delete most previous metaphors. Did someone mention a nip in the air, considering this the most significant signal among all those colours?

Knowledge What Knowledge How

That knowledge how is. Acquiring a description is not the same as feeling inside. When you were first taught it means righteous you-know-what. K4U. The highlight is a blueprint for unknowingness. Apprehension is on the tip of the tongue of how. No thirst is quenched by rote. Swimming in a deep cold sea, perfect arm strokes and sublime feet kicks, no perception of drowning. Where on this arc is knowing of the afterlife? After his unimaginable pain, three wise friends came to advise, but their agendas were mired in philosophical poles. Greek translations may get lost in the inclination.

All Good Things Must Pass

So my hot rod with its blowing head gasket but top down on this fine end-of-summer day has got to go. The quaint crop of home-grown vegetables arrive and disappear. Internet discussions unravel the Latin equivalent ad infinitum. Idioms come and go too. A run-of-the-mill would be having to say goodbye. How a data interpretation test can link such a passage from Deuteronomy to a supermarket chain. Nothing gold. Unless you sign up for that online *How to be Luckier* course, free until the subscription sets in as its own irony. There are twenty scriptures exploring things passing away, yet not one about faith. Thank you George.

Shrinking in its Moment

Inversely to Poincaré, what if our awareness is proportionate to a decrease observed? If you put your head in the laundry and wash. Sitting at the roadside, viewed by cars that have passed you by. Don't be ageist. When polymer chains lose their energy. That existentialism before a bubble bursts. Seeing the cultural landscape of this island diminish to less. Inversely again, there is explosion. Writing the narrative to its littleness. So many rises and falls. Considering all variables in the equation, and especially an existence of external torque, we can infer our star is shrinking. With decreasing amounts of money to buy reducing space.

Soothed

To use *use smoothed* is enough for feel and delineation. Pathos in harmony. Bringing the healing power of a message to misspellers. The work of vowels in *allay* and *lull* and *calm* and, if lesser so, *demulcent*. Fifty ways to soothe your lover. As a label, the antonym for what it cures. Submit your soothing images here: . That was the gentlest one.

Not That Song

You would have to have believed to think a blasphemy by singing it there. Remember if another instead how easy it is to confuse sounds for what history has made them. Without a chorus this is all narrative devoid of judgement. Imagine mistaking what was being played when you wore that baby blue and I was less concerned with colour. The airplane flying overhead is just blast even though it's mainly metal. Breaking a heart is really possible. Etherised under a table by blandness. You can't always play what you want, though some rednecks do. Lamont has every right to make those songs new-beautiful. Ohrwurm crawling the wrong tune.

Cloud Clarity

Almost as it sounds. How diamonds have heavily bearded girdles more intriguing than cumulus definitions. Unlike the real ones that hide things. With Halloween approaching, prayer partners are seeking lucidity on the potential for darkness in formations. Beyond, where the blue is always clear, there are flaws not easily noted. Electracy of the Cloud as literacy for the sky's future. *Fog / gloom / mist / puff / smoke / vapour / veil* are not synonyms for clearness. Hospitality suite in the firmament. There is online advice on how to tart up your tiresome cloud pics.

By Shaming

There are those who will participate in anything that allows dissidence. The moon knows. Hope is the lesser focus of preaching. I do not listen but I hear it all the time, she claimed. Are there really fine lines? The righteous harassment of politicians and other philistines. A charter for cruelty. Data walls. The dark comedy of correction and the most used word in a dictionary. All judgement balances the weight of being wrong. Find it driving into a town on signs like advertisements. Could a skywriter hurt with such inherent size but transience? Powerful medicine. A dark night of the soul can have impermanence too. To call it *reverence* is such a strange concept. Devil is in the detail.

Unwittingly

To our extinction, though many had been drawn predicting pictures in red and black. Where culpability gets a pass. *Sometimes You Just Can't Win.* Accomplice to a willingness for being confused. Some fittingly dubious echo in the rhythms of escape and anonymity. Unknowing in a stasis of calm so innocent there would be no need for a visitation even when angels existed. An elephant in the room might have walked there on its own. All the illumination for reading at night and yet the sky can no longer see its nocturnal narratives. How unwitting sin is prompted by one unwittingly cultivated before / or as George Jones once sang it.

Substitute

It is only fanciful if you believe it is surreptitious. Who? How we are still unable to acknowledge the unexplained, even if trolls are a technology for the blind. There are many who know political shapeshifting has gone awry. *Oh baby, baby, baby – how I used to love U*. When we do not want the original returned. Swaplings who barter before intuition. The self-discovery of oaf wiedersehen. Angel within. Wavering is not an imposture like the tide has no uncertainty. Howl and owl are never interchangeable but can be confused in wishful hearing. As Coleridge danced and sang with them, he knew happiness was changed forever.

Inside a Cloud

To cool a cloud of its atoms is to swagger in the atmospherics. An artist who makes indoor clouds has discovered the texture of transience. Is it a cult of our new technology to store such faith inside the Cloud? Swelling and thickening and rolling and sculpturing invisibility of vapour. A realistic rendering of clouds has an abstract. This twee metaphor of bed sheets in the sky. You can fly a plane directly into and along yet only words shape within and with. Anisotropic here too – scattering – and future mash-ups are being mapped as I compose. Thank you George.

Taking out the Trash

For sanitation purposes, we have that euphemism, but don't get me going on an analysis of *recycling*. There are those who believe this is a gender issue. On the days when politicians want to bury their dead. Removal of an unwanted, carried like a capture of disease in expectant stench and snake eyes. Sonic landscapes of trash. Is it because of my age I undertake this chore and do not understand the memes? Reject the illusion: one person's detritus will also be another's. The number of lyrics that show there is no lyricism in this.

If the Door is Closed

There are deductions to be made. Behind every one is a finite world waiting to be lived. If you knock, consider how this could pre-empt an existential moment, as clichéd as such would be. When privacy settings were the lack of ajar. This cause-and-effect nonsense of another opening. As for gods shutting them – surely deities have ironic devils to push and seal? Hanging down with Charlie. When it is a two-status deal, nuance is either locked in or out. *Door open alerts come when door is closed*: thank goodness this world is so fucking crazy.

Isolation

In that suggestion for discipline, advice seems oblivious to the void of solitude. What does it look like / like looking for what? When one becomes another of nothing. People who are not friends will never know better than what we expected in our initial disappointment. It is all about choice, as the diatribe goes, but when pathways are awry there is only the circuitry as it is. You isolate the source to repair, but when this is yourself, there is a symmetry that cannot roll. Like Bukowski's dice, if you want exemplification. There is much on *virtue* and *joy* out there. Evolution in the experience of being remote and content. When there are six new shoots of pampas grass, this can be enough in a lonely part of the garden.

Waiting for Anything to Come Along

You wander into a charity shop, like turning at the wrong corner, and there it is, on the floor, no higher than you would ever have dreamed, and only scuffed down the right-hand side. Is it selfish to expect more, as if not enough is too little? Another fable about a bus. Imagine coaxing is another form of coaching, laying the bait of anticipation to train for hanging around. Did it say let us lie in wait for the blood moon as if this defined our innocence of not knowing? Statistically, the longer you do, the nothing must be as much as the anything. At some stage, darkness will saunter by. There's always Godot. And the four gospels.

Blue Trees and a Pink Thunderbird

Let's promote a discussion about juxtaposition. Being real, gliding across a desert you'd want a hardtop and air conditioning. If only destruction was this pretty. Crayola childhood. A streetscape hue cruised by another. There are those who might think blue trees are allied to the angels. Confidentially, kinda neat and sweet. Beyond but planted in the earth. If Gauguin's seem alien, these are as natural as the sky. Havana hues too. Would apples be that colour as well? The trees should never be twelve-bar, but the '57 could carry like any blues guitar. Uncanny that he sang with the Blue Caps. If approximations, one interprets and transforms.

www.ingramcontent.com/pod-product-compliance
Lightning Source LLC
LaVergne TN
LVHW041304080426
835510LV00009B/862